S.H.W.A

Minority Economic Advantages

By:

El Ahkenon

S.H.W.A

Minority Economic
Advantages

Published by Krystal Lee Enterprises (KLE Publishing) Copyright © 2025 by El Ahkenon. All rights reserved. Please send comments and questions:

Krystal Lee Enterprises
770-240-0089 Ext. 1
sales@KLEPub.com

To Reach the Author:
Email: raylavario28@gmail.com

Printed in the United States of America.

ISBN: 979-8-89987-908-1

Disclaimer

The information contained in this writing is for educational purposes only. Nothing contained herein is intended to be legal advice or to be construed as such. This presentation is designed to provide information regarding the subject matter covered. It is provided with the understanding that the author is not engaged in rendering any legal services or expert assistance.

Services of a competent professional should be sought when applying the information herein. Readers are urged to read all material, research, and learn as much as possible about the subject matter herein, and to tailor information to their own individual needs. Every effort has been made to make this information as complete and accurate as possible. The information has been obtained from many sources in regards to these professions.

The author believes everything in this book to be moral, legal, and ethical. I do not profess to be an attorney or specialist in regards to the content herein, nor the statutes, laws, codes, or regulations regarding these laws, statutes, codes, or regulations. The task to learn and apply this information is up to you. Hope you all enjoy and experience new prosperity in the days to come.

S.H.W.A

Minority Economic Advantages

Table of Contents

Introduction

This book is written with the intention to bring about financial therapy for all who suffer from a superficial and physical state of poverty. It is written in human terms, so all who read it can learn, understand, and be enlightened in the many ways to obtain financial prosperity.

Within the pages of this book reside loopholes and secrets created by the government. These loopholes and financial secrets have created millionaires and even billionaires. However, this book is not written for those who lack vision, imagination, tenacity, faith, hope, coordination, and a sound mind. If you possess the above characteristics, understand the power of knowledge, and the application thereof, you will find the information herein of great value.

This book is specifically aimed at corporate entities, businesses, and individuals who interact with commerce on a daily basis. Many people do not understand commerce, not to mention the true meaning and essence of what money is. Yet, we interact with 'commerce' using 'Money' daily, unconscious of what is going on. This unconsciousness of 'commerce', and misconception of what money really is, is part of the cause of mass poverty throughout our nation. One must not only grasp an understanding of what money is, but must also obtain an understanding of the laws that govern the multiple concepts of money.

We must understand money and commerce from a professional standpoint. I'm not saying we have to become professionals to deal in commerce, only that we must view money and commerce the same way the professionals do.

I can almost guarantee that once you are equipped with the knowledge contained in this book, your financial situation will change drastically. In your hands is the information that makes a little bit of money go a long way for those who apply it.

Lawyers, Accountants, CPAs, Securities Brokers, Mortgage Brokers, and most friendly politicians will charge you an arm and a leg for applying this information on your behalf. This may be the only book you need to accomplish your goals as swiftly as possible. No one wants to be broke, homeless, and not knowing where their next meal is coming from. Ignorance has created dependents and functional illiterates who unconsciously interact in commerce for the sole benefit of making money. Let's put on our goggles of awareness, so that we can save and make money as we interact in commerce and delight daily in our own prosperity.

This book includes actual contracts and forms to assist anyone who chooses to apply the information herein. This is not a "get rich quick" book, nor are any "get rich quick schemes" contained herein. This is 101 assistance literature. Please enjoy. REMEMBER, TIME IS MONEY.

Welcome To Prosperity

Chapter 1: Money

We have grown up all our lives believing we know what money is. Some have worked to their graves for the mighty dollar. People have committed horrendous acts to obtain it. Nations have subjected other nations for the love of it.

The mighty dollar has become God to many. Those born in less fortunate circumstances and those born with the platinum spoon in their mouth. These poor individuals have become obsessed with the illusion that having enough money can solve any problem that occurs.

Poor, financially challenged individuals exchange huge amounts of labor (energy), working for minimum wage for multi-billion dollar companies without fully understanding the true nature of the exchange. For some, the circumstances are so pressing and demanding, that they do not want to understand the true nature of the exchange; they just know they need the money. But have you actually sat down and asked yourself, what is money?

What is this that I'm chasing day and night, in-time and over-time, as you punch the clock daily. But what is it even? Take a moment to reach into your purse or wallet and pull out one of these good old dollar bills. Any bill will do. Examine the bill.

Pay close attention to the words written on it. At the bottom on each side of the face of the bill, you will see two signatures. If you look in the upper left-hand corner, you will see a clause that says: "THIS NOTE IS LEGAL TENDER FOR ALL DEBTS PUBLIC AND PRIVATE." There is also what appears to be a tracking number in the upper right and left-hand corners.

It is detrimental that you know what the mighty dollar bill is and the role of law and trust that regulates it. We are going to break the mighty dollar bill down in great detail to its base essence in a brief moment. But before I do this, I would like to present to you an expert point of view of... "What is money?"

I'm no expert, but there's nothing like an expert point of view. It is always highly recommended that an expert can better deliver to an unsuspecting mass of individuals a transparent understanding of his or her profession. Therefore, I take it upon myself to introduce you to a very important piece of information from an expert in regards to what money is.

Have you heard of a workbook called Modern Money Mechanics? You probably haven't. It is a book about bank reserves and deposit expansion, written by the Federal Reserve Bank of Chicago.

Now, who can tell you better than the Federal Reserve Bank about what money really is? The Federal Reserve Bank is our expert right now. And I quote from the expert in regard to what is money:

"What is money? If money is viewed simply as a tool used to facilitate transactions, only those media that are readily accepted in exchange for goods, services and other assets need to be considered... Today in the United States, money used in transactions is mainly of three kinds:

Currency (paper money and coins in the pocket of the public); Demand Deposits (non-interest bearing checking accounts in banks); and other checkable deposits such as Negotiable Orders of Withdrawal (NOW) accounts, at all depository institutions including commercial and savings banks, saving and loan associations and credit unions.

Travelers checks are also included in the definition of transaction money. Since $1 in currency and $1 in checkable deposits are freely convertible into each other and both can be used directly for expenditures, they are money in equal degree. However, money held by the non-bank public are counted in the money supply...."

"This transaction concept of Money is the one designated as M1 in the Federal Reserve stock statistics. Broader concepts of money (M2 & M3) include M1 as well as certain other financial assets (such as savings and time deposits at depository institutions and shares in money market mutual funds) which are relatively liquid but believed to represent principal investment to the holder rather than media of exchange. While funds can be shifted fairly easily between transaction balances and these other liquid assets, the money creation process takes place principally through transaction accounts...."

It is only proper to receive an expert point of view of what money really is. If you read Modern Money Mechanics even further, there resides a very important topic about "What Makes Money Valuable?" I quote:

"In the United States neither paper currency nor deposits have value as commodities. Intrinsically, a dollar bill is just a piece of paper, deposits merely book entries.... what then makes these instruments—checks (book entries), paper money and coins—acceptable at face value in payment of all debts and for other monetary uses? Mainly, it is the confidence people have that they will be able to exchange such money for other financial assets and for real goods and services whenever they choose to do so...."

According to our expert point of view regarding "What Is Money," we have learned that there are three kinds of money:

i. currency (paper money and coins),

ii. Demand Deposits (non-interest-bearing checking accounts), and

iii. Negotiable Orders of Withdrawal (NOW)

accounts, as well as travelers checks.

Money experts refer to these three kinds of money as "transaction Money" or M1. In addition, our expert tells us that $1 in currency and $1 of checkable deposit are money in equal degree and can be freely converted,... well easily converted into each other and can be used to purchase merchandise and services.

Being that our Money expert "specializes" in Money, we must not take it lightly when it is stated in regards to "what makes money valuable" that "neither paper currency nor deposits have value... a dollar bill is just a piece of paper, and deposits are mere book entries."

This may be shocking and confusing to many individuals who are uneducated and unlearned in the Money Field. However, our bankers, Securities Power brokers, Hedge Fund Managers, and many Chief Financial Officers know the true nature and value of money. That mighty dollar bill is just a piece of paper and once it is deposited with a bank or any financial institution, it is converted into a 'book entry'.

Now before we go any further, I would like to clarify this: 'transaction money' consists of 'paper money', coins, checkable deposits, and NOW Accounts, which is considered and viewed by the Money Specialist as 'money held in the pockets and purses of the public'. The Money professional also referred to these monies as instruments.

So when we ask our professional what makes the money valuable—it states it is the confidence people have that they will be able to exchange such money for other financial assets, real goods and services whenever they choose to do so. It is the confidence to exchange for goods and services and financial assets that gives value to money—

without this confidence to exchange, our paper money and deposits, according to the Money Experts, are simply paper and 'book entries, or, in other words, WORTHLESS! Transaction money (M1) is defined as such because it is 'ready' to be exchanged for goods, services and financial assets.

Remember, there are 3 types of money and we were only referencing M1 money. There is also what is known as M2 and M3 Money, which is considered by our Money Specialist to be a broader concept of money, such as 'commercial paper', time deposits, savings deposits, stocks, shares, money market mutual funds, bonds, and convertible notes. This money is 'relatively liquid but believed to represent investment to their holders and not transaction Money. As aforementioned, M2 and M3 Money is not transaction money that is ready to be exchanged for goods and services.

M2 and M3 Money must be "gotten ready" or 'made liquid' before it is converted into 'transaction Money' (M1). M2 and M3 Money goes through a conversion process on a daily basis and can be easily shifted into transaction book entries. The Internal Revenue Code has specified provisions for tax purposes where transactions or exchanges are conducted using M2 and M3 money as a 'Medium of Exchange' or 'Medium of Settlement'.

Don't be concerned about the legal terminology being used at this moment. When you put down this book, you will realize that you are surrounded by money on a regular basis. You will have a full understanding of the legal terms used, and how effective they are when being applied.

You will know and understand how to create your own money legally and lawfully. Did you know that in the United States our government does not mind if you choose to 'create' your own money? That's right.

The Federal Reserve Banking System as established in the United States is designed to allow the people to create their own money for the benefit of the people as well as the banking system itself. As you should know, counterfeiting money is out of the question and against the law. Anyway, who needs counterfeit when you can legally 'print' the real deal.

Let's put our professional goggles on and turn our attention back to Modern Money Mechanics regarding a particular portion about "Who CREATES MONEY?" It is nothing like hearing it from the professionals. And I quote:

"Changes in the quantity of money may originate with actions of the Federal Reserve System (the central bank), depository institutions (commercial banks), or the public (people). The major control, however, rests with the central bank. The actual process of money creation takes place primarily in banks.

As noted earlier, checkable liabilities of banks are money; these liabilities are customers' accounts. They increase when customers deposit currency and checks and when the proceeds of loans made by the bank are credited to a borrowers' account... banks can build up deposits by increasing loans and investments, so long as they keep enough currency on hand to redeem whatever amounts the holders of deposits want to 'convert' into 'currency'. This unique appearance of the banking business was discovered many centuries ago...

It started with goldsmiths, as early bankers. They initially provided safekeeping services, making a profit from vault storage fees for gold. People would redeem their deposit receipts whenever they needed gold or coins to purchase something and would physically take the gold or coins to make payment.

The recipient would then deposit them for safekeeping, often with the same banker. Everyone soon found it was much easier to use the deposit receipts directly as a means of payment. These receipts, which became known as 'notes', were acceptable as money since whoever held them could go to a banker and 'exchange' them for metallic money.

Then bankers realized they could make loans by giving their promise to pay (or bank notes) to borrowers. In this way, banks began to create money... transaction deposits are the modern counterpart of bank notes. It was a small step from printing notes to making book entries, creating deposits of borrowers which the borrower in turn could spend by writing checks, thereby printing their own money...."

As mentioned earlier, the quantity of money changes and can be affected by and through actions of the public, the central bank, and depository institutions. We now see that it is the public and the banks who have control of the money creation process. Just as the banks create their own 'banknotes' to be used as transaction money, so can the 'public.'

Understanding that checking deposits are merely book entries or information transcribed in a book, designated in a specific person's name, regarding this individual's financial transaction; one could freely become aware and understand the nature and essence of money. Deposits are book entries and dollar bills are simply 'bank notes' that can adjust a transaction account in a negative or positive manner.

When you are writing checks against a 'deposit account' held at a bank or financial institution, our professional says we are 'printing our own money.'

Once an individual comes into the true knowledge of money, they will begin to respect the power of pen, paper, and knowledge as great assets when properly applied. The people or public have the power and financial right and freedom to determine how much money will be created to circulate or be exchanged in commerce. By law, it is illegal and unlawful for anyone to re-print Federal Reserve Notes WITH THE INTENT to exchange them for goods and services. The FEDERAL Reserve Bank is a private corporation that controls the United States monetary system. Our dollar bill is a 'Note' created by a 'private corporation', which has been adopted and accepted as transaction money which is ready to be exchanged for goods, services, and financial assets.

This information being presented is being presented from a professional's understanding, knowledge, and perspective. I am not a Money professional, but the FEDERAL Reserve is. Also, by obtaining a professional's knowledge and understanding of money—what it is, how it is created, and how it is made valuable—we may be able to apply that information like the professionals when conducting ourselves in commerce and the financial community.

The public can create money, and the public makes money of VALUE. And by writing checks, we print our own money... think on that for a minute. While you are thinking, I want you to take a good look at that dollar bill you took out of your pocket. Yeah, the green corporate note. In the upper left-hand corner resides what our money professional refers to as a 'conspicuous clause'. It reads as follows: 'THIS NOTE IS LEGAL TENDER FOR ALL DEBTS PUBLIC AND PRIVATE.'

The conspicuous clause describes the dollar bill as a NOTE. So it is fair to say that this worthless piece of paper that has no intrinsic value, that we use as transaction money to purchase goods, services and financial assets, is referred to on its face as a NOTE... The conspicuous clause further states that the Note is 'legal tender'.

A lot of individuals who are unlearned in money and commercial law (commerce) have never heard of the term, yet they are well known to the money masters, and worthy to be placed on trillions of dollars now in circulation. So not only is the dollar bill a NOTE, it is also 'legal tender'. Now you would like to know what legal tender is, wouldn't you?

Well, according to our money professional, Legal Tender is our mighty dollar bills circulating as transaction money. It's written right on the face of our dollar bill. However, you may want to know what the term 'legal tender' means. We are not going to waste time looking in web dictionaries.

We are going to the professional's dictionary at this instant. This will provide us with a professional's understanding regarding the term 'legal tender'. The following definition is taken from Black's Law Dictionary (Abridged 10th Edition), Page 1023:

LEGAL TENDER

"All coins and currencies of the United States (including Federal Reserve notes and circulating notes of Federal Reserve banks and national banking associations) regardless of when coined or issued, are legal tender for all debts public and private, public charges, taxes, duties, and dues... 31 U.S.C. § 5103"

In the second definition of legal tender it 'states':

·   "Sellers of goods may demand payment by legal tender but he is required to give an extension of time reasonably necessary to produce it...."

Before we proceed, we must get a full understanding of the word 'currencies' as used in the above definition of legal tender. We are still in Black's Law Dictionary at Page 205:

CURRENCY

"Coined money, and such bank notes or other paper money as are authorized by law and do in fact circulate from hand to hand as a Medium of Exchange (Transaction Money) for all debts, public and private, public charges, Taxes, Duties, and dues, and sellers of goods can demand payment by legal tender. The key is 'Other Paper Money... Authorized by law.'"

You need to understand the power of a conspicuous clause and how to apply such tactics in this book. If you're serious about money, you will continue to read and digest the information herein.

Do you remember what the "other paper money"

is? Most, according to our money masters, that "other paper money" that is authorized by law to circulate from hand to hand as legal tender or currency is M2 and M3 Money. Which consists of Letters of Credit, Certificates of Deposit, Bonds, Stocks, Bills of Exchange, Notes, etc... What our Money Professional and the definitions regarding legal tender and currencies are telling us is that All Money (Transaction Deposits and Book Entries) - M2 Money - is designed to appear and circulate as Money to settle debt obligations public and private.

Now, hold up one minute. In a retail setting, we can't take a stock certificate into Walmart and purchase goods with it. No. Walmart has a procedure in which an individual who wishes to purchase goods must approach the checkout line and exchange "money" for the goods they wish to purchase. Yes, they give the person at the cash register cash, checks, credit cards, debit cards, cashier's checks, money orders—you know, All Money. Keep in mind, M2 and M3 Money must be made ready to be converted into full transaction money?

Yet, that does not stop it from being considered as currency nor from circulating from hand to hand to satisfy debt obligations. M2 and M3 Money IS LEGAL TENDER AND MUST BE TENDERED (offered) as transaction Money, and once accepted, debts are satisfied. If "Accepted" as transaction Money, goods and services can be purchased as well.

That's right, I may not walk inside a Walmart and purchase goods and services with that stock certificate. But I can pay a DEBT I owe Walmart IF I TENDER LEGAL TENDER (Stock Certificate) for Full and Final Payment of Debt, and if said Legal TENDER is Accepted By WALMART FOR THAT PURPOSE.

When participating in commerce or conducting commercial transactions as described above using M2 and M3 Money, there are Rules to the Commerce. Legal TENDER has Rules that Govern this type of Money.

That's right, money is governed by rules and laws, and commerce is too. You must know of and understand these laws and rules to be effective in your commercial and business transactions. These Rules And Laws are what I call the 'Rules Of The Game'.

It is a must that you understand and know the rules of the game. Can you imagine LeBron James, one of the greatest basketball players of his time, not knowing the rules of the game? Believe Me, without knowing the rules of the game, you cannot effectively participate.

It wouldn't matter if you wouldn't even make the team because of your lack of knowledge of the rules and how to play the game. It is obvious that you are in the right profession once you grasp the many concepts of money and learn and apply the fundamental laws that govern it. You can become the LeBron James of Commerce, and if you're a business owner, you can be doing numbers larger than the Lakers.

I mean literally dealing in the millions, becoming an instant millionaire overnight, by printing our own money just as our monetary system has designed it. We are seriously equipped with Legal Tender. Remember what our money professional told us, that when we write checks we are printing our own money.

Now that's how the public creates and prints their own money. Money IS CERTIFIED. You will write it on a piece of paper, and you are the one that gives that piece of paper value. Let me give you an example. The bank creates money using a reserve. Pay close attention because you can use this same Money Creating Process.

Let's say we set up our own Bank, and Jim comes in and deposits $10,000 (cash). Thus, we create a Book entry for Jim called a Deposit Account. Then Larry comes to our bank for a loan. How much of the $10,000 can we lend Larry?

Of our $10,000 in Reserve, we are required to put 10% of Jim's money in a non-interest-bearing account at the Federal Reserve bank just in case Jim comes in and wants $1,000 of his money. I can lend Larry $9,000 of Jim's money. Instead of giving Larry cash, we open up a checking account in Larry's name. (Thus creating a book entry in the sum of $9,000).

There is now $19,000 in the bank.... Jim's bank account states $10,000 and Larry's checking account $9,000. There were no Federal Reserve Notes even printed, only "Deposit Slips" THAT EVIDENCE or "Deposit Entries Being Made".

Now let's say a new customer comes to our bank, Lynn. She comes to borrow money as well. We have lent to Larry all of Jim's money that we are allowed by law to lend. So we go to the money that Larry has in his checking account, which has $9,000 in it. We lend to Lynn $8,100 of LARRY'S MONEY.

Now Lynn has a checking account at our bank in the amount of $8,100. Larry and Lynn will write checks to people and companies when they are out shopping buying cars, goods, services, and financial assets. These people and companies will deposit the checks (bills of exchange) in their bank. Before the checks even clear, our bank creates new reserves against which those banks can lend money.

This is exactly what's going on when you go and deposit your notes and checks with your bank. Your banker creates a 'book entry' in your name. And this book entry is an 'asset' to the bank, as well as a liability.

A Bank's liabilities in this particular relationship are that the bank owes an individual for making a deposit. Banks keep what is known as a Double-book entry concerning that particular transaction: one entry for assets, the other for liability. In financial accounting, this is known as the "accrual method of accounting." There are rules that govern this 'book entry' accounting method regarding an individual's financial transactions.

One of the reasons why the banks and other large financial institutions keep these 'Double-book entries is to keep up with the money they owe individuals for making deposits. That's what Credits represent, remember. When you make a Deposit with the bank, You Are Actually 'Lending' the bank money (checks, Notes). A form of transaction takes place.

You have created what

is known as a Creditor-Debtor Relationship whereby you are the creditor because you lent to the bank by making the deposit. And the bank is the debtor because it accepted your note or check as a loan and, in exchange, gave you a Promise to pay you back on Demand. Trust me, many individuals do not know this. Only because they have not been educated in the business of banking. Any time you are opening or making a deposit into a checking account or certificate of deposit, you are participating in the business of banking.

When you enter a bank and tell them you want to open a Deposit account, you are actually telling the Bank, "I want to lend you some money." Right now, as I told you earlier, I am not a money master or Professional. I only wish to enlighten you from a professional point of view and present to you a professional understanding so that you may become a professional in your own time and dealings.

There are some really great professionals out there who have written very enlightening information about their professions, especially when it comes to Business transactions regarding commercial law. These guys are professors; they have PhDs in their Professions and have dedicated many years concerning these issues and others in their Profession. It's a Book I Have in my Personal Library called Modern Business. This is a Book that instructs an individual on the Rules Of The GAME as it relates to Doing Business in Commerce.

In this book, there is a Specific portion that explains what is actually going on when we make these Deposits at the bank and the relationship that is created once these deposits are made. And I quote in Part:

"When we open up a deposit at a bank, people

honestly think that they have money in the bank, which is so far from the truth. What really is going on is that the individual has lent the bank money and the bank has promised to pay the individual back on Demand."

"Thus creating at the bank a 'DEMAND LIABILITY.' The individual has become a creditor to the bank and the bank has become a debtor to the individual..." (Thus creating a CREDITOR-DEBTOR RELATIONSHIP.)

So if the bank goes bankrupt with your money on deposit, by law, as a creditor to the bank, you will have a claim against the bank for that amount. What a relationship? That's right, your business relationship when you open a deposit is that you are loaning the bank money and not actually depositing money in the bank as most think they are. This type of relationship is "CREDITED" in many different business transactions where money,

goods, or services is loaned to another whereby the lender expects to receive legal tender (money) at a later time.

The bank ledgers the money you loan them as an asset because they accepted it as such. That's why the bank in the above illustration was able to lend Jim's money to Larry, because Jim loaned our bank his money; we could do whatever we want with it. So the bank is accepting paper money (bonds, rebates) as assets and liabilities evidenced by book entries that are known as 'Deposits,' which by law is considered as a loan, which is being kept in Double book entry form.

Banks also have other departments that deal with M2 and M3 Money. Believe me when I say the banks do not turn down any money you wish to lend them. They accept not only your transaction Money but also your bonds, Notes, and Stock Certificates.

Now that you know what money is, you know the relationships you have with your bank when opening an account (deposit). You may have come to the realization that you have more money to lend the bank than you think. In our illustration, 10% of Jim's money was placed in a reserve, allowing our bank to create money in 'book entry form.' T

he more money banks hold in their reserve, the more money they can create to lend others. I think your eyes are beginning to open now. You might want to revise that old business plan or revisit those business ideas that you have built in your mind's eye. Like I have spoken of banks, they have different sorts of branches and departments to receive the money you wish to lend them by opening up deposits.

For example, if you walk into a bank and try to open a checking account using a stock certificate, the teller might tell you, "I don't 'accept' that, I'll need cash, check, or money order (money of equal degree)." Debit cards will be accepted as well. However, if that bank has a 'securities department', the teller will politely direct you to that individual department that 'specializes' in this type of money.

Say Danny runs this division. He approaches you and asks, "How can I help you?" You tell Danny, "Yes, I'm trying to open up a 'checking account,' but I only have these Stock certificates, promissory notes, and bonds." "No great," Danny says, "come on over to my office and I'll need you to sign the appropriate 'contracts' to establish your account."

What Danny may do, seeing that he is a "Securities Broker," is open you up a "securities account" that will simply allow you to write checks against the Securities you just deposited. These securities are lodged as assets and liabilities as well and evidence money owed to you as creditor. Remember, M2 and M3 money are not ready or intended to be converted into transaction money (dollar bills) immediately. They have a market where this paper money is sold, and through sales, it is converted into dollar bills. And this is going on all day and night on a daily basis where this other paper currency is circulating from hand to hand as satisfaction, assets, and payments for debts public and private.

M2 and M3 Money

In the beginning of this book, our money professional at the Federal Reserve Bank told us that M2 and M3 money are broader concepts of money which include transaction money as well as certain other financial assets (such as saving and time deposits... and shares in money market mutual funds). Shares are stocks, whether they be common stock or preferred stock of a corporation or voting trust. Financial assets are Long-term Notes, bonds, stocks, Long-term Bills of Exchange, commercial paper, options, futures, Repurchase Agreements, Mortgage Backed Securities, Futures contracts, etc... The list could go on and on.

You would normally view money of this kind circulating on the Nasdaq, New York Stock Exchange, and other money markets abroad. Nearly every developed and developing country has a "money market." Trillions of Dollars in M2 and M3 money are bought and sold daily.

It is worthy to mention that a vast majority of our money in the U.S. is in book entry form representing credits and debits (assets and liabilities). Companies, Corporations, Limited Partnerships, Real Estate Investment Trusts, and other entities make and issue their own M2 and M3 money that is then sold as financial assets on these money markets throughout the world. We have been mainly programmed and conditioned to believe that the mighty dollar bill is the only money that can be authorized for goods, services, and financial assets. You must realize and understand that the laws of the United States are made for our benefit also—to allow us as a people (the public) of the United States to print and issue our own money is perfectly legal. Yet, due to a lack of understanding and professional knowledge regarding What Money Is, we have become ignorant in our view towards money and do not understand the Power we possess as MONEY CREATORS.

We spoke of that special Creditor-Debtor Relationship established once you walk into your bank and open a deposit. Well, the bank loves when individuals come to their establishment to loan them money. Who wouldn't love that? Understanding this relationship and your ability and power to create money will allow you to use that information to benefit you and others, especially your banker or Financial Institution.

As spoken earlier, the majority of banks have Securities divisions or affiliates that specialize in Securities (M2/M3 MONEY). And they all allow you to come in with your own SELF-CREATED INSTRUMENTS for the sole purpose of opening or making a Securities deposit. When you open an account by depositing Securities at these places, you are lending them your Securities (Money or Financial assets). In exchange, they promise to pay you on demand in 'like kind'.

We are not even going to focus on the exchange at this moment. You give them money, and they give you a Promise to pay! However, this is what's actually going on when you are conducting the above transaction with a brokerage house. I'm giving this to you straight from a professional standpoint so that you may benefit from the Creditor-Debtor Relationship and your ability to create money. This is how the majority, if not all, of these securities companies operate when dealing with stocks, bonds, notes, commercial paper, debentures, and so on. This is coming from the LAW as it pertains to the Securities business as conducted today!

I quote:

"This section recognizes the reality that as the securities business is conducted today, it is not possible to identify particular securities as belonging to customers as distinguished from other particular securities that are the firm's own property. Securities firms typically keep all Securities in Fungible Form and may maintain their inventory of a particular security in various locations and forms including 'book entry' positions at one or more clearing corporations...."

According to law, it is not possible to identify particular securities as belonging to customers. The reason for this is that when customers deposit these securities with their securities brokers, the securities are held in 'Fungible Form' (co-mingled). Simply put, Fungible Form allows the broker to co-mingle the securities of its customers and use them as the Securities Firm's assets; they are or become collateral/assets of the Securities Firm.

Once deposited, the customer is given what is known as a margin account credit. Margin account credits work also like checking accounts. They simply match the value of the securities you placed on deposit with the security firm. Many of these security firms will provide you with checkbooks and debit cards to access that margin account credit that is held in book entry electronic form. The Securities firm, once in possession of this

M3 money, then uses the securities as collateral to obtain loans for themselves. Actually, they hypothecate these assets.

Hypothecation is simply using other individuals' collateral or assets that have been delivered to your possession as collateral for a loan without actually delivering or losing possession of the collateral itself. If the Security Firm goes bankrupt or belly up, you will have a claim against the Firm for the amount of the securities held on deposits. In the event you demand your securities back once they are held in fungible form, you will only receive payment in like form of a check.

What I take about these security accounts is that they allow you to play the MARGIN GAME. Nine times out of ten, when you open a Securities account by depositing securities, you will sign what is known as a margin agreement. The term "margin" simply refers to

using borrowed money to make an investment. The margin account is used to purchase stocks.

I'm going to make this simple for us all by allowing the money professionals to explain how this works. His name is Ken Kurson; he wrote The Wall Street Journal Complete Money and Investment Guidebook. He explains how this MARGIN thing works. And I quote:

"Under current rules, most stock purchases require at least 50% down up front, which means half of the purchase can be done on margin (or by using borrowed money). So if you want to purchase $10,000 of Microsoft stock, you need to put up only $5,000 in cash to purchase that stock. This means your broker is lending you the other $5,000 and charging you interest on their loan while you hold the Microsoft shares.

A more common and riskier form of margin is USING STOCK YOU

ALREADY OWN AS COLLATERAL THAN CASH TO BUY STOCK. Here's how this works: you have $5,000 in MARGIN ACCOUNT SHARES. You want to buy $10,000 of Microsoft shares. You can use the equivalent of $5,000 in MARGIN ACCOUNT SHARES to satisfy the $5,000 cash margin requirement..."

Playing the margin game is perfect for "money creators" due to the fact they can use their own self-created stock certificates to cover the margin. We are authorized by law to create our own stock certificates for margin requirements and to deposit in securities accounts, which will change the substance of our money from paper to electronic book entries representing credits and debits (assets and liabilities). We are just touching bases at this moment. You will be given a step-by-step process to apply this information.

The key is to get you to understand what money is and your power as a "Creator of Money." Once you realize you are money, you will then notice that you are also surrounded by money everywhere you go. Once you recognize this, you are almost ready to participate in commerce as a professional.

We are going to take a brief moment to focus on the Creditor-Debtor Relationship and how it works in commerce. This relationship is the foundation of all commercial transactions. It is a must that you understand this relationship.

Chapter 2: The Creditor-Debtor Relationship

In the business world, there are two types of individuals: Creditors and Debtors. A Creditor is a person or entity to whom money is owed. A Debtor is a person or entity that owes money to another.

This relationship is created when a person or entity lends money, goods, or services to another person or entity. The person who lends is the Creditor, and the person who receives the loan is the Debtor. This relationship is created by contract, either express or implied.

An express contract is one where the terms are stated in words, either oral or written. An implied contract is one where the terms are not stated in words but are inferred from the conduct of the parties. In commerce, the Creditor-Debtor Relationship is the most common relationship.

It is the foundation of all commercial transactions. When you go to the store and purchase goods on credit, you are creating a Creditor-Debtor Relationship. The store is the Creditor, and you are the Debtor. When you take out a loan from a bank, you are creating a Creditor-Debtor Relationship.

The bank is the Creditor, and you are the Debtor. When you deposit money in a bank, you are creating a Creditor-Debtor Relationship. You are the Creditor, and the bank is the Debtor. This relationship is governed by the Uniform Commercial Code (UCC), which is a set of laws that govern commercial transactions in the United States.

The UCC provides the rules for creating, enforcing, and discharging the Creditor-Debtor Relationship. It is important to understand this relationship because it is the key to understanding how to use money and commerce to your advantage. As a Creditor, you have certain rights and powers.

As a Debtor, you have certain obligations and duties. By understanding these rights and obligations, you can structure your commercial transactions to benefit you. For example, as a Creditor, you have the right to demand payment from the Debtor. You also have the right to charge interest on the loan.

As a Debtor, you have the obligation to pay the Creditor according to the terms of the contract. You also have the right to dispute the debt if you believe it is not valid. The Creditor-Debtor Relationship is a powerful tool in commerce. By understanding how it works, you can use it to create wealth and prosperity for yourself and others.

Chapter 3: Creating Your Own Money

Now that you understand what money is and the Creditor-Debtor Relationship, you are ready to learn how to create your own money. As we have learned, money is simply a medium of exchange. It can be in the form of currency, checks, or book entries.

It can also be in the form of stocks, bonds, notes, and other financial instruments. The key to creating your own money is to create a financial instrument that can be used as a medium of exchange. This can be done by creating a promissory note, a bill of exchange, or a stock certificate.

A promissory note is a written promise to pay a certain amount of money to a certain person at a certain time. It is a negotiable instrument, which means it can be transferred from one person to another. A bill of exchange is a written order from one person to another to pay a certain amount of money to a third person.

It is also a negotiable instrument. A stock certificate is a document that represents ownership in a corporation. It is a security that can be bought and sold on the stock market.

To create your own money, you can create a promissory note or a bill of exchange and use it to pay for goods and services. However, for the note or bill to be accepted, it must be backed by something of value. This is where the Creditor-Debtor Relationship comes in. You can create a promissory note that is backed by your own credit. Your credit is based on your ability to pay your debts.

If you have good credit, your promissory note will be more likely to be accepted. You can also create a promissory note that is backed by collateral. Collateral is property that you pledge to secure a loan. If you default on the loan, the Creditor can take the collateral. To create your own money, follow these steps:

1. **Establish Credit**: Build a good credit history by paying your bills on time and managing your debt responsibly.

2. **Create a Financial Instrument**: Draft a promissory note, bill of exchange, or stock certificate. Make sure it includes all necessary information, such as the amount, the parties involved, the date, and the terms of payment.

3. **Back It with Value**: Ensure your financial instrument is backed by your credit or collateral. This gives it value and makes it more likely to be accepted.

4. **Negotiate It**: Use your financial instrument to pay for goods and services. Negotiate with the other party to accept it as payment.

5. **Honor Your Obligations**: If your financial instrument is accepted, make sure you honor your obligations. Pay the debt according to the terms of the instrument.

By following these steps, you can create your own money and use it to participate in commerce. This is how the professionals do it. They create financial instruments and use them to conduct business. You can do the same.

Chapter 4: How To Contract

Knowing how to contract is important. It's almost like an art or a sport. Practice makes perfect, so you must perfect it by constantly creating and presenting OFFERS TO CONTRACT.

The contract is a very important document. Bankers, Salesmen, and all persons in the business of providing goods, services, and financial assets establish their transactions according to the terms provided in the Contract. And you better believe these contracts are created to work in their favor.

In a court of law and equity, the contract is evidence of an agreement between both contracting parties. The contract evidences the full meeting of the minds as to the terms set forth in the contract. Your signature evidences that you fully understand the terms of the contract and accompanying Documents and are satisfied with the terms.

Not all contracts require Signatures. These contracts are called Simple Contracts. You are going to learn what I call monster contracting in this Chapter.

Many individuals are so excited to obtain that beautiful residential property that they'll sign the contract without reading the terms, for which they have obligated themselves for the next 15-30 years. Millions of consumers do this all the time. And many unheated businesses do as well.

But not the professionals. What do the big boys like Donald Trump, Warren Buffet, Apple, and Dell do? They read the contract first so that they may understand the terms down to the last sentence. And if the contract is adverse to their liking, they'll present a counter offer with terms that favor them.

This is known as a Counter Offer. This is standard procedure when making a deal. Before the deal is consummated, you should have time to go over the whole contract and any accompanying documents. When you know how to contract and negotiate the terms, you should be able to make any contract work in your favor when you apply the information from herein. You can even make adverse contracts work in your favor.

There are all types of contracts, and they all have legal names to describe them, such as:

1.   ORAL CONTRACTS
2.   WRITTEN CONTRACTS
3.   EXPRESS CONTRACTS
4.   IMPLIED CONTRACTS
5.   UNILATERAL CONTRACTS
6.   BILATERAL CONTRACTS
7.   VOID CONTRACTS
8.   VOIDABLE CONTRACTS
9.   EXECUTED CONTRACTS
10. EXECUTORY CONTRACTS

A formal contract is embodied in writing and under seal. But other contracts are simple or informal.

I will now allow you to reduce the same information that I have from the professors of Modern Business. I advise everyone to have a copy of this book, not only Entrepreneurs. I want to recant what these professionals and professors had to say about contracting:

"The importance to the business man or the professional man of putting his agreements in writing can scarcely be overestimated. Avoidance of misunderstanding and subsequent litigation are the results since proof of the written contract is a matter of certainty. Put all the terms of the undertaking in black and white and there can be no contract verset..."

According to the professors of business and commercial law, the written contract is to avoid any future controversy that may occur as to the terms of the contract. Implied Contracts are those in which, from the circumstances and nature of the transaction, the facts imply a promise; conduct takes the place of words and no signature is required. For example: Sending goods in response to an offer to contract is an acceptance of the offer to contract which is contained in the order; an acceptance implied from the offeree's conduct.

EXAMPLE:

Say you mail your offer to contract to B, specifying the terms in which the offer to contract is to be accepted and attach a check marked with a conspicuous clause that evidences the acceptance of the check is full satisfaction of the thing you are offering to contract for. B accepts your offer and deposits the check but refuses to send the merchandise. B's acceptance is IMPLIED by the depositing of the check (conduct). You now can enforce the terms of your offer to contract in a court of law or equity, in which the court will command B to perform to the terms of the contract and deliver to you the merchandise you tendered the offer to contract for.

ANOTHER EXAMPLE OF AN IMPLIED CONTRACT IS:

Say you see a taxi or cab sitting on the curb of the road waiting. It doesn't need a specific destination. An implied contract is formed. The presence of the taxi on the curb IS THE OFFER. When you enter the taxi, that is your acceptance to pay the cost charged upon you for getting you to your specific destination.

Even when we visit a dentist, it creates a contract to pay the specific price of the visit, where no price has been specified. Then, we have contracts IMPLIED BY LAW, which are called QUASI contracts. These are also implied contracts.

Quasi contracts are simply OBLIGATIONS imposed by law to place liability where it belongs.

TERRY purchases a car from ROB for $500. The price of the car is actually $300. TERRY over pays ROB by $200. The law will implicate a promise by Rob to repay TERRY the $200 excess.

Implied contracts are significantly important to the entrepreneur who is trying to get his start-up off rock bottom and are a major tactic in monster contracting.

Then we have BILATERAL CONTRACTS and Unilateral Contracts. When you enter into an agreement consisting of a promise for a promise, you have just entered into a bilateral contract. A person promises to sell to another who promises to buy is a bilateral contract.

An Example of a Unilateral Contract is: where one person promises to pay another $300 if the other person promises to dig a hole according to a stated specification; the promise is for an act, and so is unilateral. It becomes a contract only when the hole is dug.

Contracts that have been fully performed by both parties are called executed Contracts. Contracts that are fully performed by one party but not by the other are called executory Contracts.

A VOID CONTRACT is a contract where the performance is expressly prohibited by law.

EXAMPLE:

A person cannot contract legally or lawfully to kill another person; such an act is prohibited by law.

A VOIDABLE CONTRACT is one that can be avoided by a party thereto.

45

An infant under the age of 21 can back out of a contract at any time, thus making the contract voidable due to his infancy.

It is a must that you know how to contract like the professionals when conducting your business and legal affairs. I am not just referring to reading the terms of a contract before you sign it. I'm referring to putting together your own contracts regarding the thing you desire.

By doing so, you will know and understand the terms of the contract. Your initial offer to contract will be the foundation of the contract or the transaction. Any counter offers will address the terms set forth in your initial offer-to-contract; therefore, you will not be lost regarding terms that your contracting party wishes to alter or re-negotiate.

Do you know why banks, lenders, and car dealerships hit you with those 50-page small print contracts? They do it to create as many loop-holes as possible for their benefit. The shorter the contract, the more air-tight it is, and the easier it is to interpret. There is no wiggling room at all.

Banks and lenders have prepared standard contracting terms when conducting their business affairs. These lenders also provide extraordinary contracting terms when transacting with those they call their 'executive clients'. Executive customers receive five-star services, custom-made to accomplish these business objectives. Knowing how to contract reveals to your banker that you are a serious business man. When you combine your contracting skills with your knowledge of money, investments, and how to properly utilize corporate entities, they will more than likely consider you a potential executive client.

When these lenders

contract with you, they are trying to obtain from you as much VALUE as they can possibly get, in the form of RIGHTS.

What are RIGHTS? Well, according to our professional Black's Law Dictionary, the term RIGHT MEANS:

"... giving to the term a justice content, a right is well defined as a capacity resulting in one man of controlling with the assent and assistance of the state, the actions of others; ... a power, privilege or immunity; ... in a narrower significance, an interest or title in an object of property, a just and legal claim to hold, use, or enjoy it, or convey or bequeath it, as he may please; A legally enforceable claim of one person against another, that the other shall do a given act, or shall not do a given act...."

SCAN ME

Call or Text:
770-240-0089 Press Extension 1
Web: KLEpub.com
Email Services@klepub.com

It's time to start and finish   **YOUR Story**!

KLE Publishing specializes in helping people become authors. In as little as 15 to 90 days, we can help you develop your books and e-books and publish to 39,000 outlets! We also offer audiobook services.

Write, Edit, Format, Publish
We can help from
Start to Finish.

Explore and learn more about published authors affiliated with KLE.

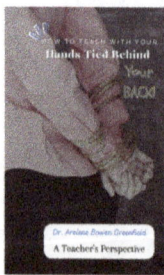  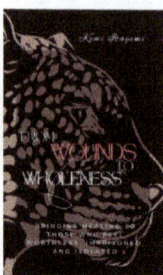  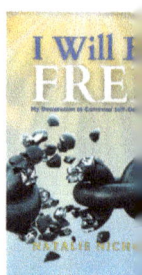

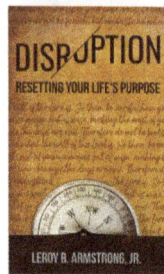 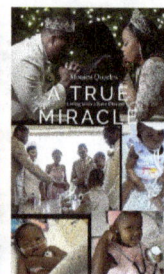  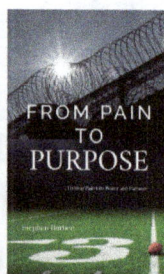 

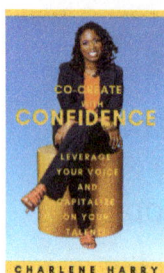  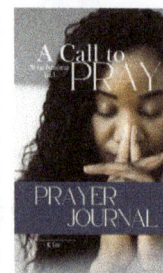 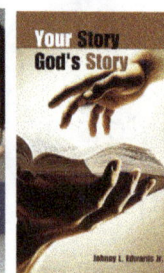 

   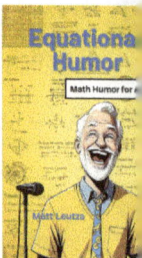

KLEPub.com